Migizi

by
Guillermo Bosch

Published December, 2012
Fallen Bros. Press
6010 South Pacific Coast Highway #9
Redondo Beach CA 90277
ISBN: 978-0615763118 (Fallen Bros. Press)

Author's note: *While "Migizi" was inspired by actual events, it was undertaken as an experimental "anti-epic" poem for the author's MFA thesis. The story itself is a fable, and not intended to be a documentary of persons living or dead. The characters and situations are solely the products of the author's imagination.*

The verses of the poem are meant to be sung and accompanied by music while the "Ein besinnliches Zwischenspiel" to be chanted.

Acknowledgements must be given for the invaluable advice and encouragement of Bosch's thesis advisors, Jane Wohl and Elena Georgiou. Further heartfelt appreciation for the inspiration and spiritual friendship of Thirza Defoe.

Illustrations from Hieronymus Bosch (c. 1453 - 1516)
Cover and interior design: © Guillermo Bosch, 2012

For all the birds…
sacrificed.

CONTENTS ....Page

1. The Miraculous Migrations of Exotic Birds............................1
Ein besinnliches Zwischenspiel...3

2. A Historiography of Afghan War 7
Ein besinnliches Zwischenspiel...9

3. The Ephilei of Birds of Paradox...13
Ein besinnliches Zwischenspiel...15

4. The Transubstantiation of an American Warrior 19
Ein besinnliches Zwischenspiel...21

5. The Eventual Numbing Effect of Unimaginable Deaths........27
Ein besinnliches Zwischenspiel...29

6. The Cognitive Influences of Jealousy
on Early-Life Expiration 35
Ein besinnliches Zwischenspiel...37

7. An Unmentionable Incident at Dawn's Early Light...............43
Ein besinnliches Zwischenspiel...45

8. The Irresistible Attraction of the
Flawed and the Maimed 51
Ein besinnliches Zwischenspiel...53

9. On Mitigating Guilt Through Unconditional Love 59
Ein besinnliches Zwischenspiel...61

10. Great Acts of Valor Often Go Unnoticed 67
Ein besinnliches Zwischenspiel...69

11. The Consummation of An Unknown Warrior's Journey.......75
Ein besinnliches Zwischenspiel...77

Glossary of References 83

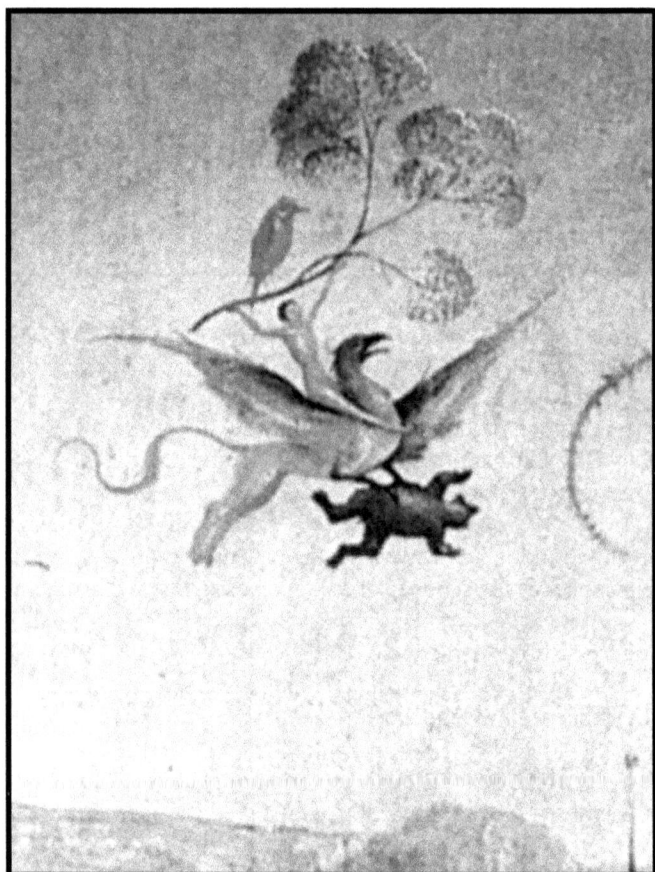

Migizi

1. The Miraculous Migrations of Exotic Birds

Great Speckled Bird, harassed and hectored,
despised by swarms of Satan's flocks,
by crimson Angels of Destruction,
by false Gods bringing endless war.

Your virgin feathers brush my skin,
your sharp beak pricks my silent lips,
you sweep sharp grit out from my heart.
I'm losing the fear I cannot fly.

Almighty Bird, born Seraphim,
your clarion call raised in alarm
has power over Langley's agents,
exposing killers from The Farm.

So set me free to tell this tale
of shattered limbs, of mucked up brains,
of ghostly dead who point toward me
as they stalk the fog lands of my dreams.

Angelic Bird spread out your wings
that we may soar into fierce skies
from concert halls to sweat-soaked fields
inhaling scents of fighting men.

We're forced to nest near roaring flames,
in mountain passes stripped of green,
in cities plundered, brought to rubble
where all have fled to stony caves.

We'll smell bleak blood of dark-eyed children,
the crimson tide from the thousands dead,
rust-red blood of weeping daughters,
the clotting blood of camouflaged souls.

We'll hear lost war's weary echo,
the crumpled trucks, the deadly drones,
the bullets' splat as they strike bones,
the muezzin's evening call to kneel.

We'll sing about warrior Migizi,
cruel fate's choice for a sacrifice,
denied true love, reduced to murder.
We'll wonder how he found his way.

Bird of Peace, fly here near me.
We'll set our course for Afghanistan.
But we must rise with fading day
before this darkness overwhelms…

Ein besinnliches Zwischenspiel #1

At sunrise, chill autumn air mists
valleys of the towering Hindu Kush,
where a long-legged
White Siberian Crane steps
carefully, walks with
deliberation, along
the shrinking shore
of Lake Ab-i-Estada,
her young one
huddled nearby.
Behind her scarlet mask
eyes dart, dip, flicker...
No male to carry on
shimmering Siberian dances
learned on summer steppes
outside Yakutsk. No male
to raise the danger call, to draw
the devil dogs away.
No male
to protect her child.

Her jealous gaze catches
orange and pink Flamingos
breeding in throat-filled passion,

Guillermo Bosch

tiny brown and white
Kentish Plovers playing
bird-tag through swaying reeds,
Slender-Billed Gulls singing
French-African songs
from Senegal.

Our White One does not sing.

New birds fly
the routes of her migration,
metal feathered,
metal-winged,
naked in their form
and their intent.

The mother brushes her neck along
her child's neck.
She ruffles outstretched feathers.
At 18:00 hours,
mother and daughter rise
toward tangerine setting sun.

There will be no more
White Siberian Cranes
on Lake Ab-i-Estada

over the Hindu Kush
in Afghanistan.
No more.
Never.
None will return.

Guillermo Bosch

2. A Historiography of Afghan War

Our tale begins, October 7
in Christian era, 2001,
as wheeler-dealers gorge on greenbacks,
and shameless preachers bless our greed.

We're in that time when W. rules
with billowing flags and counterfeit cross.
He's fattening banks and corporations,
while bloated bodies burst in floods.

As America sleeps, faint Crescent moon
sheds waning light on Eastern lands
where fedayeen bend down on rugs
worn thin from wind and gritty sand.

Beneath their knees, lie lakes of oil,
which fuel the fires of our Western hearth,
while refugees have unlit stoves
in grim cold caves and tattered tents.

So Allah's warriors gaunt and sullen,
their eyes sucked dry by desert winds
feel Qur'an words ring in their ears.
They call for jihad, Enshalah!

Guillermo Bosch

In mud-walled huts, their plans are made.
In wind blown tents word passes on.
In fetid slums the danger deepens.
As the century dawns their plot has jelled.

Four hijacked planes dive from the clouds.
Two strike New York; twin towers fall.
Steel and glass rain from fierce fires.
Bodies plunge through ash-filled sky.

As we watch those towers crumble,
as we see three thousand pay
in sacred coin which wants revenge,
we call for death to heathen hordes.

In public chambers of our Congress
lawmakers give us Total War.
They swear to wipe out Jihad's warriors,
to cleanse the earth of murderous men.

Afghan peasants hear the rumbles.
As they run out from mud brick homes
missiles roar above their mountains.
The stench of death. The shock of war.

Migizi

Ein besinnliches Zwischenspiel #2

We might have begun with
"Once upon a time not long ago,"
yet in fact time must go
further backward toward
long, long ago…
long, long before Oetzi Man, wounded
by arrows, sat dying,
then frozen in Alpine glacier
in Sud Tirol, long,
long before painted horses appeared
on walls of caves
beneath Lascaux, long,
long before sacrificial heads rolled
down Tenochtitlan altars, long,
long before Shoshone
hunted buffalo,
before Cheops' pyramid rose
in the Giza necropolis, long,
long before Nebuchadnezzar raised
Hanging Gardens in Babylon, long,
long before the Zhou, before Shang, even
before the Xi Dynasties, long
long before Koga Ninja
performed their secret kills and long,

long, long, long before Twin Towers fell,
Paktha farmers settled
the Arghandab Valley
near Deh Morasi Ghundai
(now, Kandahar), a place
chosen
for pomegranates, almonds
and poppies
but not for people
planted there
smack dab along the routes of
the conquering armies:
of Cyrus the Great,
of Alexander the Great,
of Seleucus (was he great?)
of Demetrius, (not so great)
of the Great Seljuq,
of Genghis Khan (must have been great)
of Queen Victoria, (imperiously great)
of Leonid Brezhnev, (brownbearly? great) and
George W. Bush (ingrate).

Back, back through time
(and forward now?)
into this valley tucked
between the Hindu Kush and Sulaiman.

Migizi

How many mud-baked towers,
how many towers built from cypress wood,
towers built from Lashkar Gah stone,
how many blue-tiled minarets
how many golden domes
have fallen?
How many Pashtun, Tajik,
Hazara, Parziwan souls have
risen?
Or descended?
There.

Here. A lone peregrine
father sweeps
above soot strewn urban canyons
his mate gone, their eggs
shattered
but truth be told,
in American hearts
no foreign deaths
or un-hatched eggs
can match
steel towers gone
or even one
fair-haired child
turned cold.

3. The Ephilei of Birds of Paradox

At old Fort Drum near Sackett's Harbor
on land once held by Iroquois,
Mountain Men of the Airborne Corps
gear up to fight in Jingly Land

One giant warrior, born Ojibway,
was raised with tribal songs of war,
of dead Dakota, Fox and Cree,
killed to fuel the White Man's greed.

His mother, Chepi, hated legends
which glorify all those who died.
She remained barren many years.
She swore she would not make a son.

But one fall night in a sad blue yearning
feeling adrift over life's lost dreams,
she makes love to a tall bald eagle
who plants a seed inside her womb.

So one gray dawn in Minnesota,
Leech Lake awakes to a baby's cry.
At dusk, crazed Chepi climbs grass mounds
which cover bones where ancients sleep.

She holds her son toward the purple sky
and chants a curse upon the boy:
She prays her son will be a she-male
with curly hair and pouty lips.

But Chepi's curse has mixed results:
Her son is strong, not soft nor weak.
His arms are tight as rolled coiled steel.
He grows to over six foot six.

And while his face is very pretty,
and no hair sprouts on his massive chest,
his soft brown eyes do not disguise
the angry scowl on those thick curled lips.

As Migizi grows, his anger hardens.
He beats up bullies in Bucktail's Bar.
He badly bruises a First Trust banker
who tries to steal his mother's home.

Soon brazen boy, his head unbowed,
stands uncontrite before Judge Gould
who demands Migizi rot in prison,
or join the men going off to war.

Migizi

Ein besinnliches Zwischenspiel

Nothing is as
it appears to be
in conjured Kingdom of Daruny
existing out of space
(east of Switzerland,
west of Austria,
south of Germany
north of Italy)
and time,
only in a yearning
boy/girl mind
sculpting
an enchanted dot com,
a cyberspace palace,
a funhouse play
for those unattached,
for those unseen
who pass through lonely
convoluted triangle,
man's Adam's apple, Adam's
rib as well
into hell
-ish confusion.

What is gender meant to be
if nothing is as we see?
1798's "Hey! rub-a-dub,
Ho! rub-a-dub,
three maids in a tub…"
becomes 1830's
"Rub a dub dub,
Three men in a tub…"
Even for Mother Goose
things change from one thing
to another, you see.

See more:
Male Ochre-bellied Flycatchers
mimic female calls,
attracting other males.
See mallard drake
on the make
in his egg-less club
on blue Leech Lake
where above calm waters
eagles glide
through rain and pale
gray sky so high
we cannot watch
the love they're making.

These eaglemen,
brothers to Ishtar,
Summerian God of War,
brothers to Griffin Ahura Mazda,
Zorastrian God of Wisdom
brothers all,
warrior brothers,
bent,
but not broken
have sharpened talons
to tear,
rip, and kill
at will
when tormented.

They also rest
at peace in nest
with chosen mate,
accepting their fate
as they raise their throats
in evening rainbow call,
earth lullaby,
for delighted denizens
of Daruny.

4. *The Transubstantiation of an American Warrior*

And so Migizi trains in weapons.
He fights in heat and bitter cold.
But unlike Zeus, he has no lover,
since Army men can't touch nor tell.

Still he is drawn to his Ganymede
a slight young man with golden hair.
They call him Blue for his azure eyes.
He's also Doc, a medicine man.

Their team is lead by Pistol Pete,
a hirsute brute, a villainous troll
who trembles under Blue's healing hands,
and hates Blue's soft, hesitant voice.

But Pistol Pete craves Migizi.
He loves the giant's strength and will.
He also loves Migizi's looks,
his thick full lips and dark brown eyes.

The recruits train for a Final Test,
Vulcan's Hammer, the devil's forge,
pushes men beyond their limits.
It breaks those weak; it honors strength.

Migizi and Blue are Battle Buddies.
At 40 miles Blue's ankle snaps.
Pete wants Blue left mired in mud,
but Migizi lifts Blue up on his back.

As he bears Blue 'cross swollen streams,
in shimmering heat of one hundred ten,
Migizi's tendons strain near snapping.
Veins protrude from his thick, taut neck.

Salty sweat stings his eyes.
His muscles throb, but he struggles on.
His lungs are burning near the end,
but he completes in record time.

When weary men stand in formation
proud and tall on their camp ground.
Pistol Pete gloats as the Colonel
declares that Pete's team is best.

After hoohas Pete hails Migizi,
and offers him two chevron stripes.
He shakes his hand in an iron grip,
and makes Migizi next-in-command.

Migizi

Ein besinnliches Zwischenspiel

By the sea,
young innocents toted
by doting Mom & Dad
reluctant to utter
after womb's exit
(or even inside
if vanishing twin
be sacrificed)
"strong ones
survive!"

Instead,
they encourage
chattering young
to cast their bread
on foaming waters,
into the air,
or onto the beach
toward squawking gulls
who wail
and steal.
Momma says,
"See that little
one there.

So cute. Throw
her some crumbs so
she can eat."
But as dough
lands
at gull's webbed-feet
stout bills of rangy
ornery bird
with fish hook wounds
and scars on cheek
intrude.
Craaaaack! screams
our thief and flies
away.
"Try again," good
moms will say,
only to observe once more
our avian
tragicomedy.

Along the Helmand River flowing
north of Unai Pass,
through Dashti Margo desert
into parched, polluted
watershed,
Seistan marshes,

Migizi

and salty Hamun-i-Helmand
river bed,
naiveté
need not be lost
having never
been born.

River terns are
slimmer, sleeker
gulls, numbers depleted,
scrounging survival
among rusting ruins,
and brackish waters.

Along Helmand River
there's seldom
bird strife,
so little life
left to be
consumed,
and starving children
do not throw
their bread away.

In Christian Book,
Ecclesiastics,

chapter eleven,
verses one and two
King Solomon says,
"Cast thy bread upon the waters:
for thou shalt find it
after many days..."
these verses used by
preacher men to urge
investment, so ten times ten
in returned riches
will come
to those filled
with hope
and trust
in dust.

The Qur'an says
nothing of casting
bread, but it does speak
in Yusuf Chapter 12
of carrying "bread
on my head of which birds ate..."
a few lines later
interpreted to mean:
"birds shall eat
from his head..."

which can only happen
if the prophet
is dead.

Thus be
the Words
of Gods for
tern and
gull.

Thus be
the Words
of various Gods
for all.

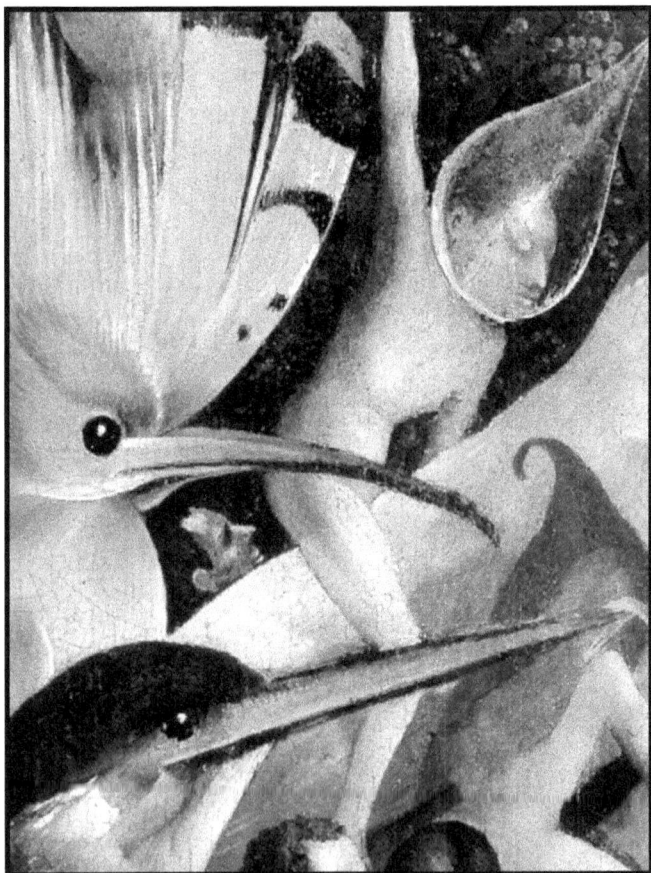

5. The Eventual Numbing Effect of Unimaginable Deaths

Meanwhile hot war begins in earnest.
Tomahawk fire and Hornet sting
are loosed on Kabul, Tora Bora,
on Jalalabad and Kandahar.

At Halloween, when ghosts and goblins
roam simple streets in US towns,
frigid winds freeze Mazar-i-Sharif
unprepared for its Day of Death.

On November 9, two months after
planes flew into New York towers
Mountain Men and Corporal Migizi
surround Chechen and Arab men.

Jihadis group in Razia Girls School
vowing to die without surrender,
so Mountain Men begin their siege
by blowing the windows to smithereens.

Through the loud night, the battle rages.
Young men scream and old men groan.
Out on the streets, the women wail
a dirge for dying boys inside.

Migizi's pulse pounds with excitement,
as he grabs grenades, and slithers across
the broken glass and sharp-edged stones
to turkey peek an unhinged door.

As he stands to reach inside
a Chechen fighter sees him rise.
He draws steel knife, slice whacks Migizi
who screams and falls with gaping wound.

Migizi's brothers focus fire
on the open door as Blue creeps out
to drag Migizi back to safety
while air jockeys fly and drop their bombs.

The Girls School is obliterated,
and all inside are sent to hell.
Migizi's medaled for his bravery,
with Silver Star and Purple Heart.

Later that night in a field E.R.,
Migizi, drugged with morphine,
dreams he feels Blue give a kiss
which makes Migizi's weak heart roar.

Ein besinnliches Zwischenspiel

Controlling air
is said to mean
controlling ground
war doctrine states
if by control we
mean shrill screams
of black, burning flesh
in Dresden (30,000),
in Hamburg too (40,000).

Giulio Gavotti was first,
the silly flying fool
who decided to drop,
on a lark it appears,
his hilarious conception,
against Turks in
Ain Zara, Libya,
November 1, 1911.
The Anatolians felt fire
descend from heaven,
not from Allah but
from Giulio as he reached
into his leather pouch,
found five grenades,

screwed detonators in,
and laughing, delivered
by airmail, no less,
uno regalo to mankind,
a *nuovo* scheme
to maim
and to kill.
Belgrade (17,500).
Tokyo (100,000),
London (43,000).

Gavotti failed.
He didn't destroy
any humans that day;
but an idea born is
an idea to go
and ever since
we've managed
to perfectly grow
this aerial embryo,
to where we do not need
Gavotti et al.
at all, since
pilotless drones
hum through the air
controlled by men

Migizi

10,000 miles away
with joy sticks
and flat screens—
a Wii all too real—
video games geared
for the slightly insane
warriors too much
in touch
with Star War days.
Shanghai (12,000),
Grozny (358),
Huế (3,776)
and Herat (1,237).

Sweet little humming
birds sucking
nectar from a scarlet flower
will dive bomb hawks
to protect their nests.
Australian black-breasted
buzzards drop rocks
on emu eggs
for a succulent fresh
feast when bored
with rotting carrion.
Indian elephants encaged

in urban zoos prove
mammalians can get into
the bombing act too
hurling from their prisons
huge piles of dung.
Now doesn't that prove
poor Gavotti got us
into some pretty
deep shit?
Hiroshima (80,000),
Nagasaki (40,000),
New York City (2,819).

Migizi

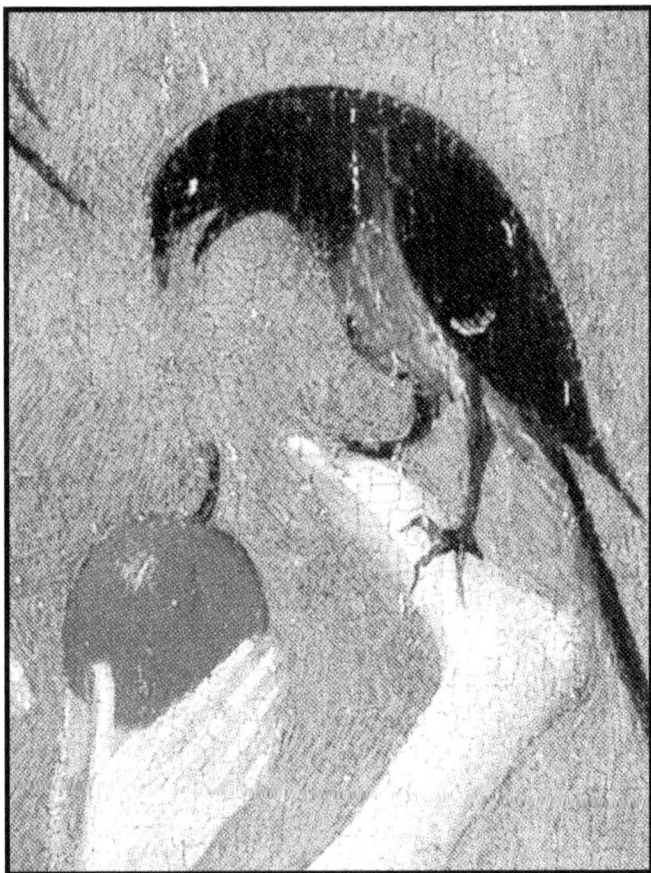

6. The Cognitive Influences of Jealousy on Early-Life Expiration

Pistol Pete's hate gnaws his guts
when he sees Blue has Migizi's love.
Pete's cheeks glow fire red hot
when Migizi brushes against Blue.

But the war goes on and our boys must kill
Ol' bin Laden who struck in hate
against New York on 9-11.
Word is he hides in Kunduz town.

So Mountain Men with Afghan allies
march to Kunduz to kill Sheik Snake.
But Pistol Pete has fouler plans
to murder Blue in battle there.

Chill dawn arrives; Migizi shivers.
He wipes dew drops from darkened goggles.
His stomach churns, his heartbeat races
as thundering explosions crush Kunduz.

Fires burn and black smoke rises
while Migizi creeps toward a shattered home.
Inside are seven Bangladeshis,
three Uzbeks, and a Saudi girl.

Migizi kills cruel Uzbek fighters.
Pete guns the Bangladeshis down.
Young Saudi girl tries to surrender.
Pete shoots her in her heaving breast.

As screaming girl squirms in her blood,
Pete calls for Blue to come and help.
As Blue works on the dying girl,
Pete shoots poor Blue right through his heart.

Pete screams and shouts, "She killed our guy!"
He then shoots into the Saudi's brain.
But Migizi knows that Pete is lying
so he savagely slits his leader's throat

Migizi hugs Blue to his chest
but does not cry as his lover dies.
His brain fogs over with dark red mist,
as he staggers out on a killing spree.

He whoops and hollers then blows away
an unarmed crowd outside a mosque.
He howls with pleasure as he mows down
three women waving a soiled white flag.

Ein besinnliches Zwischenspiel

Massacre comes from
the middle-French
for slaughterhouse,
for butcher shop,
for blood and guts
and *abattoir* gore.

We do so like to kill
our fellow man, don't we?

And the birds
as well!

In fall when millions
of songbirds fly south
to winter in the Afghan sun,
or in spring when they return
Bird Air issues
advisories not to dally
over Malta, over Crete,
over Cyprus too,
where lime sticks slathered
with thick sticky goo,
and fine nets hanging

between olive trees
lure fat birds
feasting on
golden grain.

Blackcaps and Robins
and Warblers and Finches
Flycatchers, Wheateaters
Song Thrushes and Doves
flutter their wings
in desperate defense
until snatched
from each trap
by ruthless peasants.

Clipped of their beaks,
plucked of their wings,
fried up in oil
for gourmet delights.
Ambelopoulia,
a much beloved snack
if they're not seen out front
they're hidden in back
stuffed in jars, into cans,
some wrapped in grape
leaves to disguise what

Migizi

we're eating
for five euros a piece.

One million songbirds
are killed each
season, one million songs
gone for no reason.
We'll never hear them
again on fence posts,
or tree branches,
in hayfields at harvest when
dawn light appears.

Let us weep for the deaths
of all those who sing:
for Eumolpus of Thrace
son of Poseidon;
for sweet satyr Marsyas
flayed alive by Apollo;
for Ayman Udas,
Peshwar Pashto singer
killed by her brothers
to save family honor;
for Lounes Matoub,
Algerian Berber
killed in Tizi Ouzou

for singing of freedom;
for Muhammad Jabry
decapitated in Baghdad;
for Suzanne Tamim stabbed
to death in Dubai;
for Algerian singer Lila Amar
murdered in the desert
shot in her car;
for Lennon dead on
the streets of New York;
for Michael drugged
in Los Angeles bed.

"Sing a song of sixpence
a pocket full of rye
four and twenty blackbirds
baked in a pie.
When that pie was opened,
the birds began to sing.
Now wasn't that a tasty dish
to set before the king?"

Migizi

7. An Unmentionable Incident at Dawn's Early Light

Migizi is his team's new leader,
devoured by demons of despair,
he kills Afghans without remorse.
His heart is stone. His brain aflame.

Then he is sent to Shah-i-Kot
to hunt the One-Eyed Mullah who
hides in craggy mountain caves
off tangled trails in barren rocks.

As soldiers march in eerie silence
no insects hum, no voice is heard.
Migizi senses a coming ambush
when suddenly the circle's closed.

Taliban hold the higher ground.
Mortar shells burst with harsh dull thuds.
In valley fields chaos reigns
as Migizi's men run for their lives.

Nightfall comes and fighting slackens,
but Migizi's team cannot escape.
They huddle down; they try to hide.
But shrapnel kills three bold, brave men.

Guillermo Bosch

When Migizi sees his own blood seep,
from a silver sliver lodged in his thigh,
he sneers at pain, he roars like a lion
for his men to move or more will die.

He growls for them to push ahead.
He finds a hut which reeks of dung.
His men collapse on the filthy floor,
and, exhausted, sleep on stinking straw.

Migizi stays awake to watch
At 0 dark 30, shadows approach.
He shakes his men and barks an order
to blow away those frail faint forms.

Death screams echo through the pines;
bodies fall on the stones and sand.
But bent curled horns are not the devil's.
Nor are brown eyes those of evil men.

Migizi staggers toward steaming slaughter,
hoping to savor his latest kill.
Eighteen goats are blown to pieces
and a shepherd boy lays crumpled, dead.

Ein besinnliches Zwischenspiel

Pity poor goat!
Beast of much scorn,
of Biblical slaughter,
of Qur'anic omission.

For six thousand years
goats gave their milk,
meat, skin and hair
and yet we still laugh
when they go play dead
falling flat,
legs in air
like opossums to thwart
killer's knife
waiting
at the throat.

Okay, now here's
an Afghan recipe for goat:
Take one live goat,
kill it so it's really dead,
then cut off it's head,
sew bleeding neck shut,
remove legs above knee,

sew knees shut too,
slit dead goat's belly,
remove smoking entrails,
sew up stomach as well.
Soak that dead goat in
cold water overnight
to toughen its hide.

Next day remove
carcass from water,
carry onto valley field
surrounded by men
in black and white turbans,
by laughing boys running
with tilted *taqiya*,
and horses *Turagh*,
Jarand, Samand and *Qezel*
with sweat flecked flanks,
with snot flaring nostrils ,
with hard hooves pounding,
on brown dusty ground.

Tough bearded men mount
atop their slick stallions
then form a tight scrum
inside marked chalk circle,

Migizi

where dead goat carcass
is twisted and turned
(*Buzkashi* the name for
this "goat pulling" game).
Scrum turns to brawl,
Thwak! Thwak! how fists fly,
striking on skulls
amidst curses and cries,
Crack! Crack! whips descend
across tense, straining backs,
horse's eyes bulge,
they lunge in and out,
until rider grabs goat,
explodes down dirt field,
pursued in a frenzy
by wild screaming jockeys,
whips in their hands, in their mouths
as they gallop full speed
toward the goat-carrying rider
determined to stop
him from tossing
dead goat into
goal for a victory.

When they catch
up with the jockey

they jerk him from saddle
and battle continues
on hard bloody ground
where men wrestle to mimic
hand to hand combat
which follows in war
after cavalry charge.

Buzkashi continues
through day into evening.
Sometimes a stallion
breaks away in his fright
and tramples spectators
surrounding crazed contest,
if a youngster is killed
it's just part of the game.

As night falls, the good goals
are finally counted, and
chapans awarded to
high-scoring men.
Our goat is now roasted
over open-pit fire and
bones are discarded
as men laugh and talk,
retelling past battles

Migizi

of warriors long dead
of men who fought off
those heathens so stupid
to invade their dry land.

At cool, rosy dawn
rough-legged buzzards
swoop down
to clean bones left
from last night's late feast.
The birds honor the dead beast
that ġives them such pleasure
unlike snoring warriors
who make their dead goats,
the ultimate goats
of disparaging jokes.

8. The Irresistible Attraction of
the Flawed and the Maimed

As Migizi stares at the boy's soft skin,
at empty eyes with long curled lashes
his twisted tempest tears him open,
a torrent flows from his ruptured dam.

He cradles the body in his arms,
then raises the child from blood-soaked grit.
He turns and limps back down the hillside
toward a dusty farm and a gray mud fence.

In the courtyard stands Widow Huma Hamza
whose bony hand holds her wind-blown veil
across her face to hide her horror
when she sees a monster bearing her son.

Migizi kneels before this mother;
as she collapses into the dust.
Migizi rests her son next to her.
Huma kisses her loved one's corpse.

Then suddenly from out of a hut
Shabaz Hamza runs toward his mother.
His withered arm hangs at weird angles
as he kneels down by his brother's side

Migizi shrinks from this cruel pieta
seen through his eyes still wet with sweat.
Yet he cannot help but stare
at sharp blue eyes, and the golden hair.

This Afghan boy with Slavic features,
genes implanted by a Russian rape,
this mongrel mix of stunning beauty
makes Migizi think of Blue.

Shabaz then stands, his good arm flailing,
he pummels Migizi with passionate blows
which bruise the soldier's cheeks and neck,
but Migizi does not defend himself.

When Shabaz halts his bold assault
he turns to his mother, to his bullet-torn brother.
They lift the dead boy's blank-eyed body,
to bring him back into their home.

They wash the corpse with precious water.
They close its eyes and sprinkle camphor,
wrapping the child in a clean white shroud,
they then kneel down to chant their prayers.

Ein besinnliches Zwischenspiel

Does there exist
one who can resist
a three-legged dog?
A two-headed frog?
A kitten born blind?
A broken-winged bird?

Great beauty awes
because we are drawn
to symmetry of form
wanting to believe
perfection is possible,
but perfection cannot
compete with gap-toothed
model; beauty-marked boy;
slope-shouldered warrior;
slightly bucked teeth;
bent, hooked nose;
Breasts too small...
or too large,
bow legs;
pigeon toes;
and so it goes
as it goes.

Millions have paid
to see freak shows.
Barnum and Ripley
were very rich men
who exploited freaks
like Chang and Eng
identical twins
joined at their hips—
intelligent, handsome,
and ready to please,
they gave new meaning
to being Siamese.
Zip the Pinhead,
four-legged girls,
bearded ladies,
and elephant men
were first viewed
as having
been created by Satan,
then later we saw
them as God's
special heroes.

But Afghan children
maimed every day,

Migizi

aren't freaks,
they're common,
as the desert sand.
From bombings,
and air strikes
attacks on their schools
land mines,
cluster bombs,
all take their toll.
Many don't die;
they survive their wounds—
sweet children, who cry
from Keane-painting brown eyes
walking with crutches,
or carried about,
some lying in bed
staring blankly at walls,
waifs of war
we've abandoned.
Can we seriously say
these are God's special heroes?
Or should we return
to ideas that they
are victims of Satan?
If so dare we ask
who is that Satan

who
put them in hell?

Houbara Bustard,
long-legged,
long-necked
limps on desert gravel
that stretches away
south from Kandahar
toward
wind-blown wastes
of despair.
A large silent bird,
searching for chicks,
displaced
when tough men
in brown
camouflaged 'dozers
scraped away
Bustard's home
while building
Camp Leatherneck
where Humvees roar
across flat dry lakebeds,
to hunt
warriors wandering

on camels and donkeys.

Doomed Bustard raises
its bright white tail feathers
in flamboyant display
when a rifle report!
rings in his ears
for one millisecond
before feathers fly
and he flops to the ground.

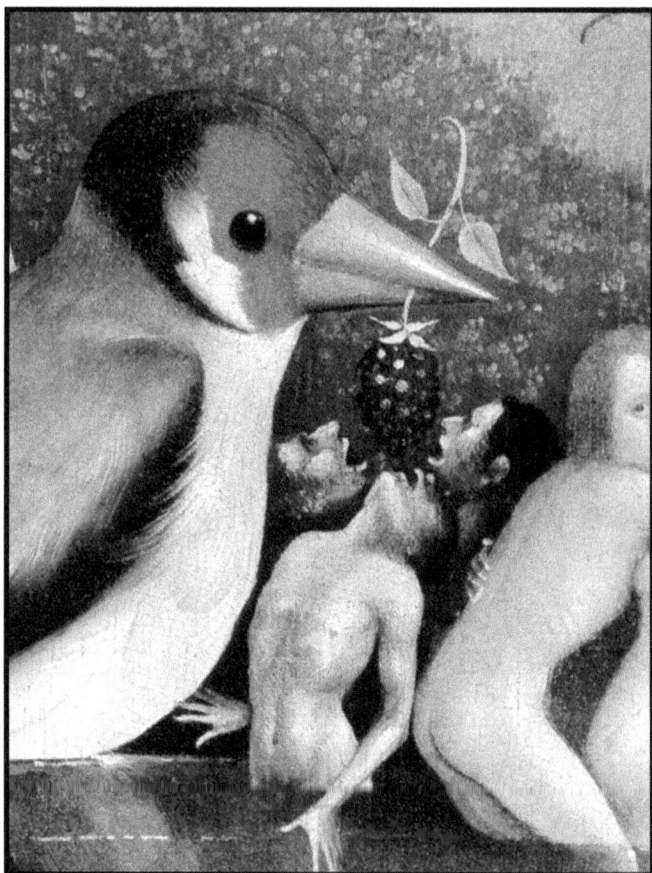

9. On Mitigating Guilt Through Unconditional Love

Migizi returns each morning at dawn.
He brings with him gifts for the sad family.
They take his fresh food and his thick warm blankets
and toss them outside on a manure mound.

When the Afghan war is declared a victory
and Migizi's team is sent to Iraq,
Migizi refuses to follow his orders
and pitches a camp on a high rocky ridge.

He buys new goats in the village market.
When Huma refuses the goat gift as well,
Migizi drives them up to the high pastures
and fattens them there on green alpine grass.

Meanwhile Huma and Shabaz Hamza
face certain starvation and untimely death
if they reject help from this man
who killed their kin and brought them down.

Perhaps if Huma were all alone
she would gladly welcome that certain death,
but she cannot in her desolation
allow her other son to die.

So Huma goes to Migizi's camp
accepting the milk, the cheese and yoghurt.
Shabaz at first won't eat the food
then he relents to hunger's urge.

Eight weeks pass and distance shrinks.
Before too long Shabaz feels free
to go with his new friend, Migizi,
to tend the goats on lush mountain sides.

As Migizi shepherds his grazing flock.
he watches the sun shine on Shabaz.
A smile transforms his brooding scowl,
his forehead smooths and his arms uncoil

But Migizi' nights are short and restless.
He's chased by phantoms he has killed.
Their shrieks accuse him of their murder
and damn him to eternal flames.

But in a vision Blue appears—
a golden light breaks his dank dark soul
and carries him back to Minnesota,
where his mother's chants lull him to sleep.

Migizi

Ein besinnliches Zwischenspiel

Bacha bereesh,
boys without beards,
are the favorites of warlords,
lords who love war and
boys, teenage boys,
whom they dress up as girls
to dance at their parties,
where the boys' twists and twirls
get warlords excited
with visions of battle
with dances of death
la petite mort confused
with a permanent one.

Bacha bazi means
boy play in English,
play which extends
past dance floor to bed
where men
who think nothing
of killing each other
tenderly cuddle young
boys in their arms and
tickle boy tummies

with long curly beards.

Zeus impregnated
many earth women
but he left them below
to bear all his children.
Ganymede he brought
with him into heaven
where he lives forever
as constellation Aquarius.

Phoebus Apollo had so
many lovers
it gets hard to follow which ones
he preferred.
But Hyacinthus was surely
one of his favorites
a young Spartan prince also
loved by Zephyrus,
swift God of West Winds,
who killed Hyacinthus
by blowing thrown discus
into Hyacinthus's head.

Bacchus loved a boy
named Ampelus, the two

swam and hunted and played
and wrestled each other.
Ampelus was foolish
one day when
he mounted
a raging wild bull
which gored him to death.
Bacchus was broken
until he discovered
Ampelus was turned
into twisting grape vine,
and so these two lovers
have given us wine.

In the bird world we know
males are privileged
with plumage, more colorful,
fuller, designed to attract
females whose feathers
remain more cryptic
better to avoid
unexpected attack.
So peacocks and cockatoos,
both strut their stuff,
while roosters fret over
which has the bigger comb.

Guillermo Bosch

Painted Buntings are dramatic
dimorphic examples
of sexual confusion
in beautiful birds,
for the colorful male,
orange, yellow and blue
looks just like a female
and fools all the others
until she/he
is two.

Migizi

10. Great Acts of Valor Often Go Unnoticed

If the Gods would just show minimal mercy
to those they throw into pitched battle
then Migizi's time on that lonely mountain
might reveal a passage to a long, full life.

But Ol' One-Eye hears about Migizi,
about a tall, strong, violent Christian
who spends his days herding short-horned goats
and watching bastard Afghan boy.

The Mullah knows this man's the warrior
who killed so many of his jihadi.
The soldier's presence is an abomination
to all who pray for Allah's will.

The Bearded One speaks to Huma
and orders her to tell her son
not to go up on the mountain
on Ashoura, in Muharram.

And so she doesn't warn Migizi,
as One-Eye's men slip through the forest
surrounding Migizi's ridge encampment
ensuring there won't be escape.

Huma does forbid Shabaz
to go that day to herd their goats.
Shabaz defies his distraught mother.
At dawn's pink light he slips away.

But Migizi knows he'll be attacked.
He's strung trip wires through the brush
and buried sticks into the ground
to warn when strangers come his way.

So as the Mullah's men approach
Migizi silently slips away
to a place where he can see them come
and if he needs to, shoot to kill.

When One-Eye signals for his men
to storm that camp where Migizi lies
Shabaz appears from out of nowhere.
His withered arm swings through the air.

Migizi knows what he must do
he does not pause to give his life.
As he leaps up to warn Shabaz
One-Eye's bullets cut him down.

Ein besinnliches Zwischenspiel

No deadly drought
nor act of war,
pollutes travertine waters
oozing out from faults
through fractured walls,
in bubbling waterfalls
crashing into cobalt blue—
into Band-e-Amir,
six lakes at over
nine thousand feet,
75 clicks northwest of Bamyan,
where silent giant Buddha
stood for two millennia
contemplating caravans
which travelled ancient Silk Roads
from Luoyang to Samarkland
then to Damascus, on to Rome,
Buddha blown away
by black turbaned Taliban
roaring across high desert
tracks in Nippon trucks
with guns attached
to pickup beds.

Guillermo Bosch

What was in their heads
to make them fear
these Buddha?

Beautiful Band-e-Amir!
where Afghan tourists go
although dirt roads are mined,
and tank turrets lie
rusting, abandoned
in nearby fields.

Beautiful Band-e-Amir!
where Afghans fish with
electric prod and tossed
grenades. Little left
for birds or wolves,
or foxes,
and what fish do remain
are filled
with mercury toxins.

Beautiful Band-e-Amir!
once wild home to tawny
solitary snow leopards
unseen for many years
around once pristine

Migizi

lakes where even
great-horned, nimble ibex,
and Turkmenian sheep herds
choose to stay away.

Ah... but wait...
One last lingering leopard
pads in cold conspiracy
toward Afghan Snow Finch nest
where gray-brown male
in black face mask
sensing the danger
hobbles out... away
from buff brown mate
and soft spotted eggs, away
from their only future hope
Afghan finches will
survive in Band-e-Amir,
hobbling, faking broken wing,
attracting leopard eyes and scent
hobbling, drawing cat away
he trips about and warbles,
out of reach but terribly near
those claws and teeth while
luring the hungry cat away.

Guillermo Bosch

Oh little finch, judge carefully
the leopard's strength,
his muscles coiled to leap.
Oh foolish finch!
Oh brave distraction!
Your action
may save your family,
but one false move
one misjudged feint...

Swiiiish, shwaaaaamp,
too late for finch,
now leopard prey...
too late...
As one soul dies
another lives,
so Band-e-Amir
may harbor leopard life
yet one more day.

Beautiful Band e Amir!
stark... harsh... lovely valley,
broken testament
to man's folly.

Migizi

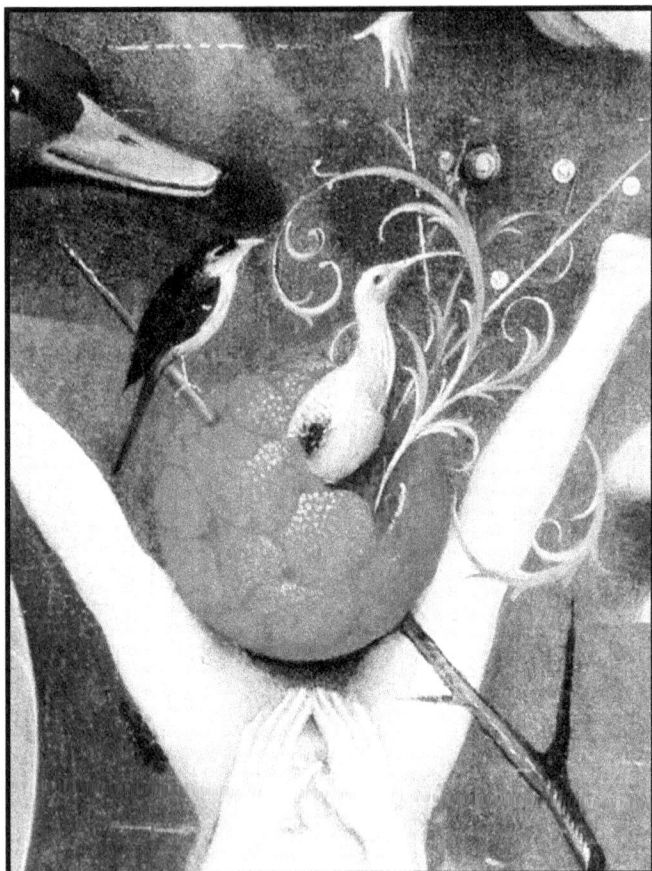

11. The Consummation of An Unknown Warrior's Journey

As Migizi lies up on that mountain
blood spurts from his deadly wounds.
As vision fades and his eyes close
he sees Shabaz or is it Blue?

One-Eye decrees Migizi's body
should stay as is on the mountainside
where vulture's beak and critter teeth
will strip flesh from his sun-bleached bones.

But when The Mullah leaves the mountain
Huma brings Migizi down
where she performs the same ablutions
she performed on her murdered son.

At dawn Shabaz and Huma Hanza
carry Migizi to fresh dug dirt.
They bury him to face toward Mecca.
then hide his grave so it can't be found.

As son and mother stare toward heaven
a spotted bird lifts from nearby pines,
soaring higher on rising thermals,
the eagle is joined by other wings:

Guillermo Bosch

A Snowfinch and a Long-Tailed Shrike.
a Black Bubil and a Baer's Pochard,
Purple Heron and Blunt-winged Warbler
Asian Flycatcher and Turkistan Tit

all hover close beside our eagle
their trembling wings aid his dying breath
as the eagle's struggle grows more painful.
they pull him in as they fly away.

They glide through clouds on western winds,
to sky-blue lakes, hills flush with bloom,
to the sweetness of green Minnesota,
they bring him home to rest in peace.

On Afghan mountain, snow dusts the stone.
The owl's head swings to find new prey.
Hush descends on evening highlands
and this night sees a new blue moon.

In Minnesota, Chepi knows
her son has left his tortured life.
As birds descend she reaches skyward
and sings her prayers for her lost boy's soul.

Ein besinnliches Zwischenspiel

Green Parrots chatter
in weeping palms,
sweet breezes blow
through white
window curtains.
Bent-back, black cats
no longer fear
the leaps and howls.
of Feckless Furies
who forced flesh
of our flesh to tremble,
to burn, to rot,
for gold, for oil
for land, for right
to rule a dying world—
this planet turning yellow,
turning brown,
not green in a
deep cobalt sea.
This big blue marble seizes
to marvel.

It's true we are a nation
growing old!

Guillermo Bosch

We stroll upon our
tar-stained beaches
where White Gulls and
Brown Pelicans soar
toward frothy foam
and seaweed shore,
where Nature's Best
granola bars,
shit-soiled diapers,
spent condoms, flattened
cans of Coke, plastic
baby bottles,
and one lonely leather shoe,
mingle within saltwater
detritus even
Magpies would disdain.

Red-tailed Hawks hunt
our sun bleached deserts,
and Vampire Vultures
circle,
promising eternal life
in return for
resignation.
Cruel coyotes bay
at a sulfur moon—

Migizi

those damnable dogs
of war who, thankfully,
cannot climb tall trees
and sink blood-soaked incisors
into nests perched
on lofty limbs, where
there are shells,
thin
from poison spread
on crops,
from poison trickled into soil,
into creeks,
into lakes,
into rivers,
into fish,
the fish then eaten
by our eagles.

Eggs precious thin,
but still alive.
There may be chicks.
They may survive.

And in our ending,
one last prayer:
Great Speckled Bird,

Guillermo Bosch

Your beak released
my silent lips,
You did sweep ash
out from my heart.
I can now fly
and
Oh My God!
Things look grand
from way
up here!

Sisters and brothers,
Procedamus in pace!

Migizi

A Glossary of References In "Migizi"

General

Migizi: An Ojibway proper name, literally, "Eagle" also "Bald Eagle" or "Golden Eagle."

Ein besinnliches Zwischenspiel: German for "a reflective interlude." In this poem, the contemplative breaks between the storytelling stanzas.

Section One

Great Speckled Bird: An obscure reference in the Biblical book of Jeremiah, 12:9, it became a reference to the Christian Church in a popular Southern hymn recorded by Roy Acuff, Kitty Wells, Johnny Cash, Hank Locklin and Jerry Lee Lewis among others. In this poem, embraced as the mythical avatar of the poet's muse.

Seraphim: In Christian angelic hierarchy, the highest rank of angels.

Langley: Langley, Virginia, headquarters of the Central Inteligence Agency (C.I.A.).

Farm: The C.I.A. training ground for field agents at Camp Peary, Newport News, Virginia.

Muezzin: The voice calling Muslim's for their five-times-daily prayer (Salat) .

Lake Ab-i-Estada: Endangered Afghanistan wetlands significant for international bird migrations.

Hindu Kush: Afghanistan's highest mountain range with peaks rising to over 25,000 feet.

Yakutsk: Siberian city in the Russian Far East.

Section Two

October 7: The date American forces began their assault on Afghanistan.

W.: American president George W. Bush.

Fedayeen: Militant fighters in the Islamic world.

Qur'an: Also Koran, the central religious text of Islam..

Enshalah: Arabic for God willing, if God wills it.

Twin Towers: The World Trade Center in New York City, destroyed in the air attacks of September 11, 2001.

Jihad: in Islam, a holy war, a religiously sanctioned war.

Oetzi Man… Sud Tirol: a well-preserved natural mummy from about 3300 BC found in the Schnalstal glacier near Hauslabjoch on the border between Austria and Italy.

Lascaux: a complex of caves in southwestern France famous for its Paleolithic cave paintings.

Tenochtitlan: an Aztec city-state founded in 1325 and located on an island in Lake Texcoco, in the Valley of Mexico.

Shoshone: An Amerindian tribe once located in the western prairies and mountains of what is now the U.S.

Cheops' pyramid: the oldest and largest of the three pyramids and one of the original Seven Wonders of the World, located on the Giza plain outside Cairo, Egypt.

Nebuchadnezzar: The Babylonian king mentioned in the Book of Daniel who constructed the Hanging Gardens of Babylon (now Iraq), also one of the original Seven Wonders of the World.

Zhou... Shang... Xi Dynasties: various Chinese dynasties from 5000 BC through 365 AD.

Koga Ninja: 15th century Japanese warriors trained in disguise, escape, concealment, explosives, medicines and poisons.

Paktha farmers: The ancient peoples who settled Afghan valleys.

Arghandab Valley: The fertile valley outside Kandahar, the second largest city in Afghanistan and on-and-off home base for the Taliban.

Deh Morasi Ghundai: The old name for Kandahar.

Cyrus the Great: Persian Emperor who invaded Afghanistan around 600 BC.

Alexander the Great: the Macedonian Greek Emperor who invaded Afghanistan around 330 BC.

Seleucus: One of Alexander's generals who re-invaded Afghanistan around 300 BC.

Demetrius: Greco-Bactrian king who invaded Afghanistan around 500 BC.

The Great Seljuq: Sunni Muslim emperor who invaded Afghanistan around 1000 AD.

Genghis Khan: Mogul emperor who invaded Afghanistan around 1210 AD.

Queen Victoria: British queen when the British invaded Afghanistan in 1839.

Leonid Brezhnev: Soviet president when the Russians invaded Afghanistan in 1979.

George W. Bush: U.S. president when the Americans first invaded Afghanistan in 2001.

Hindu Kush… Sulaiman: Major mountain ranges in Afghanistan, see section 1.

Lashkar Gah stone: a desirable stone quarried near the southern city of Lashkar Gah the capital of Afghanstan's southern Helmand Province.

Pashtun… Tajik … Hazara… Parziwan: tribal names for the Aryan peoples who settled in Afghanistan.

Section Three

Fort Drum… Sackett's Harbor: The northern New York state home of the US Army's 10th Mountain Division.

Jingly Land: US military slang term for Afghanistan, refers to Afghan custom of hanging small bells on trucks and buses..

Chepi: An Ojibway proper name, translated as "fairy" or "ghost fairy" sometimes as "dove."

Dakota, Fox, Cree: Amerindian tribes which battled with the Ojibway as each was pushed from native hunting grounds by European colonialism.

Leech Lake: A large lake in North Central Minnesota primarily located within the Leech Lake Indian Reservation.

Kingdom of Daruny: A "thought experiment" created as a fantasy web site where all citizens are recognized by whatever gender they choose to present.

Mother Goose: The name given to a country woman, the author of classic British folk tales and nursery rhymes dating back to the 1600s, most likely not one specific person.

Summeria: Middle Eastern kingdom mostly located in what is now Iraq, contemporaneous with Egypt of the pharos, known for its writing and warriors.

Ahura Mazda...Zorastrianism: Zoroastrianism is generally considered the earliest monotheistic religion. It was primarily located in Persia, and many scholars credit it as being the source for many of the concepts of Judaism, Christianity and Islam. Ahura Mazda was the supreme deity.

Section Four:

Ganymede: In Greek mythology, Zeus's male lover..

Hoohas: Military cheers given in formation, "hooooohaa".

Chevron stripes: Military insignia worn on the upper uniform sleeve designating rank.

Helmand River: Afghanistan's major waterway.

Unai Pass: A high pass in the Hindu Kush.

Dashti Margo Desert: Afghanistan's vast southern desert area.

Seistan Marshes...Hami-i-Helmand: The areas where the Helmand River empties into a marsh in Southern Afghanistan on the Iranian border.

Christian Book: The Bible.

Section Five:

Tomahawk... Hornet: US military missiles.

Kabul... Tora Bora... Jalalabad... Kandahar... Mazar-i-Sharif: Kabul is Afghanistan's capital city, Tora Bora a Northeastern mountain city, Jalalabad is an Eastern provincial capital, Kandahar is a Southern city, Afghanistan's second largest, traditional base for the Taliban, and Mazar-i-Sharif is Afghanistan's most important Northern city and the traditional base for the Northern Alliance.

Chechen men: Islamic foreign fighters from the turbulent Russian province of Chechnya.

Turkey peek: US military slang for rapid up-and-down bobbing observation mimicking a turkey's gait.

Haji: US military slang for Islamic fighters.

Silver Star... Purple Heart: US military medals, the Silver Star for extreme valor and the Purple Heart for being wounded in battle.

Anatolians: Another name for people from Turkey.

Uno regalo: Italian for "gift."

Nuovo: Italian for "new."

Wii: The video game that allows participants' body movements to control action on a screen.

Section Six:

bin Laden: Osama bin Laden, head of Al Qaeda, mastermind behind 9-11 attacks on the World Trade Center and the Pentagon, killed by US forces on May 2, 2011.

Kunduz: Northern Afghan city, site of one of the heaviest

battles of the initial Afghan War, after which battle thousands of Taliban fighters were allegedly massacred.

Sheik Snake: Slang for Osama bin Laden.

Bangladeshis...Uzbeks...Saudi: Islamic foreign fighters from Bangladesh, Uzbekistan and Saudi Arabia.

Poseidon...Apollo: Greek Gods, Poseidon, God of the sea, Apollo, God of music.

Section Seven:

Shah-i-Kot: Rugged mountain valley at over 9,000+ feet in the Hindu Kush

One-eyed Mullah: Mullah Omar, head of the Afghan Taliban.

0 dark 30: Military slang for the time between midnight and dawn.

Taqiya: Traditional Afghan caps.

Turagh...Jarand...Samand...Qezel: In Farsi, Turagh, "gray", Jarand "red", Samand, "blond", Qezel, "white" are often the names of horses in Buzkashi.

Buzkashi: Traditional Northern Afghan game, vaguely similar to polo in that it's played on horseback and there are goals, but it is much, much rougher and the "ball" is goat skin which is carried rather than struck by mallets..

Chapans: Prizes.

Section Eight:

Russian rape: The former Soviet Union attempted to occupy Afghanistan from 1979 to 1989.

Barnum...Ripley: P.T. Barnum was a famous American

showman whose traveling sideshows often contained many "freaks"; and Robert Ripley was the newspaperman who created the column "Ripley's Believe It Or Not" which referenced strange and bizarre phenomena.

Keane-painting: An enormously popular painter in the 1960s whose subjects always had unnaturally big eyes. The paintings have ultimately been attributed to Margaret Keane, the wife of the male artist who was originally assumed to be the artist.

Camp Leatherneck: A US military camp in Helmand Province, Afghanistan.

Section Nine:

Bacha Bereesh: Afghan boys used for dancing and sex by Afghan men, particularly the warlords.

Le petit mort: French for "the little death", a reference to sexual orgasm.

Bacha bazi: Sexual play with young boys.

Zeus: The most powerful Greek god, ruler of the gods.

Section Ten:

One-eye: Mullah Muhammad Omar, *see section 7.*

Bearded One: Mullah Muhammad Omar.

Ashoura, in Muharram: Ashoura is the tenth day and climax of the Islamic commemoration of Muharram which marks the martyrdom, of Muhammad's grandson, Husayn ibn Ali

Band-e-Amir: A dramatic series of lakes in the Afghan mountains and a world heritage site under serious threat from pollution.

Bamyan: Afghan Valley where two monumental statues of standing buddhas were carved into cliffs in the 500s AD, only to be dynamited by the Taliban in 2001.

75 clicks: Military slang for 75 kilometers.

Silk Road: The ancient overland trading route between China and Europe.

Luoyang: One of the four Great ancient capitals of China.

Samarkland: A city now in Uzbekistan, once famous as the central city on the Silk Road.

Section Eleven:

Mecca: The religious center of Islam, located in Saudi Arabia.

Great Speckled Bird: the poem's muse, *see section 1.*

Procedamus in pace: Latin for "Go in peace", the traditional conclusion of the Roman Catholic mass.